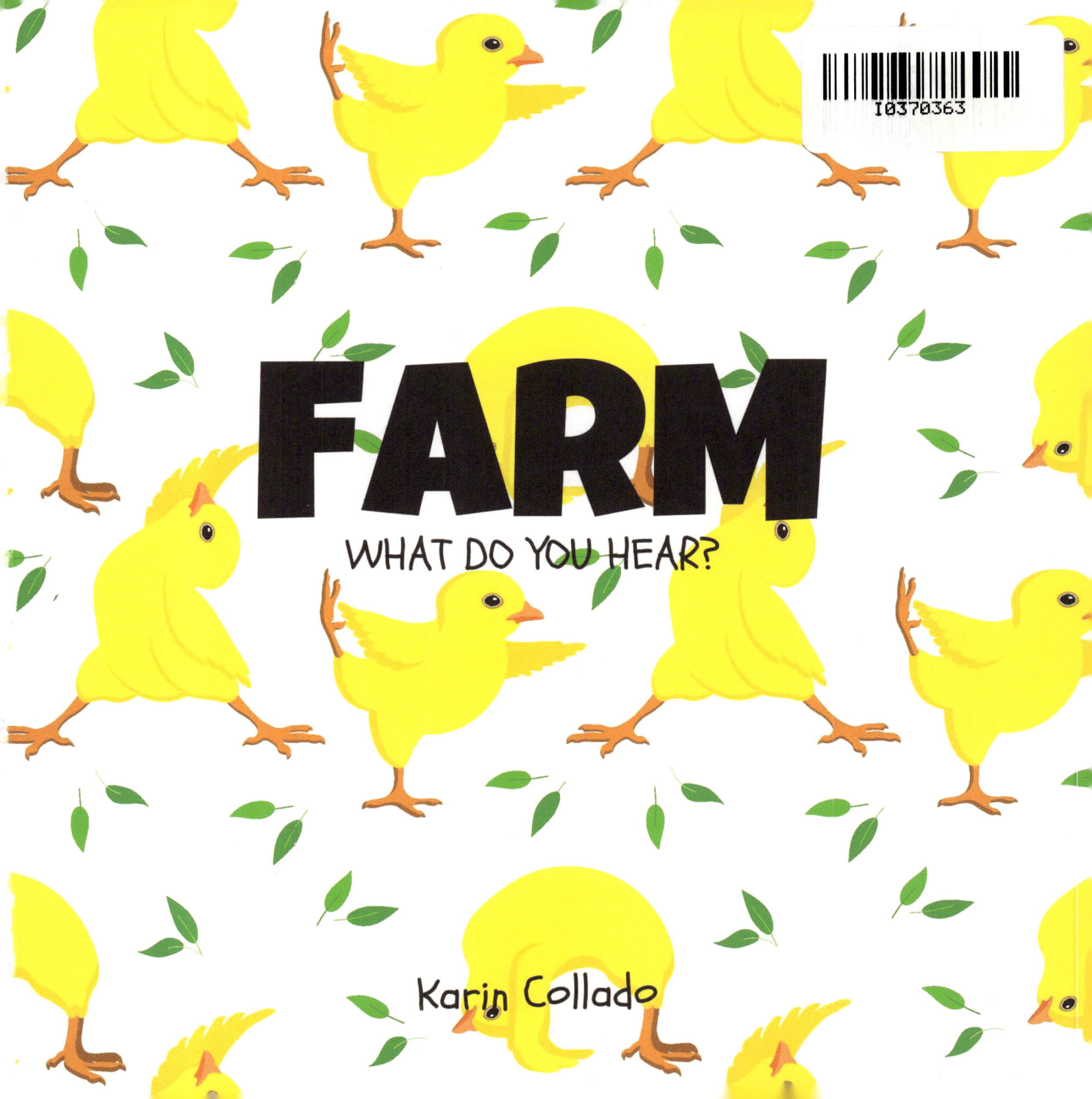

FARM
WHAT DO YOU HEAR?

Karin Collado

© 2022 Karin Collado

All rights reserved. No part of this book may be reproduced or used in any manner without the prior written permission of the copyright owner, except for the use of brief quotations in a book review.

This book is dedicated to my toddler classroom.

Oh busy farmer, busy farmer, what do you hear?

"I hear an oink, oink. Who could be near?"

It's a pig and her piglet splashing on muddy puddles. Muddy pig, muddy pig, what do you hear? "I hear a moo, moo. Who could be near?"

It's a cow and he's chewing on the grass. Hungry cow, hungry cow what do you hear? "I hear a cock-a-doodle-doo. Who could be near?"

It's a rooster and he's up early in the morning. Loud rooster, loud rooster, what do you hear? "I hear a cluck, cluck. Who could be near?"

It's mother hen and she's keeping her eggs warm. Mother hen, mother hen, what do you hear?

"I hear a baa, baa. Who could be near?"

It's a sheep and she's fluffy as a cloud. Fluffy sheep, fluffy sheep, what do you hear? "I hear a neigh, neigh. Who could be near?"

It's a horse and he's got a saddle on his back for riding. Strong horse, strong horse, what do you hear? "I hear a maa, maa. Who could be near?"

It's a goat and he's got two horns on his head. Billy goat, billy goat, what do you hear? "I hear a quack, quack. Who could be near?"

It's a momma duck and her ducklings by the pond. Splashing duck, splashing duck, what do you hear? "I hear a thumping sound. Who could be near?"

RABBIT

- Long ears
- Forelegs
- Chest
- Fluffy tail
- Hind legs

It's the pitter patter of a furry rabbit and he's got some carrots. Furry rabbit, furry rabbit, what do you hear?

"I hear noisy farm animals jumping with cheer!" Can you spot them all?

www.ingramcontent.com/pod-product-compliance
Lightning Source LLC
Chambersburg PA
CBHW042251100526
44587CB00002B/99